DATE DUE

PRINTED IN U.S.A.

I LIKE TRAINS

I LIKE

HARPER & ROW,
PUBLISHERS

New York, Evanston, and London

TRAINS

by Catherine Woolley

Pictures by
George Fonseca

I LIKE TRAINS

For Jim

I *like* trains!
All *kinds* of trains—
Freight trains,
Passenger trains. . . .

Freight trains have flat cars and box cars,

tank cars, hopper cars, and many special kinds of cars.

Freight trains carry things,

from automobiles to zebras for the zoo.

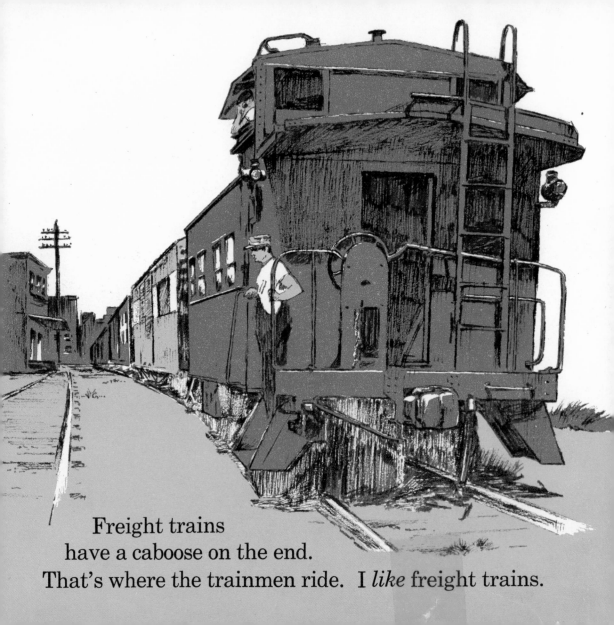

Freight trains
have a caboose on the end.
That's where the trainmen ride. I *like* freight trains.

I like passenger trains—

Express trains that rush through town on their way to far-off places.

Local trains that stop and take us on.

Some trains have a diesel engine that says, "Er, er, er, er."

Some trains have an electric engine—"Hm, hm, hm."
And some trains that don't go far have just a motor

in the front car. This motor
is so quiet that we hear the
wheels say loudly, "Clackety, clack, clack."

Trains have an engineer to drive the engine.

Trains have *very* high steps to climb.

Trains have seats to sit on—plush or plastic or cane. Some seats have a clean towel to rest our head against.

Sometimes we can turn the seat over and ride backward. We can kneel on the seat, if we want to, and look out the window.

Sometimes we can push a button
to make the seat lean back.

Trains have a baggage rack to put our suitcase in.

Some trains have water coolers. We pull out funny, flat paper cups to drink from. We get *very* thirsty on trains.

Trains have a conductor to punch our tickets.
When we come to a station, he calls, "Middle-
TOWN, MIDDLEtown. All ABOARD!"

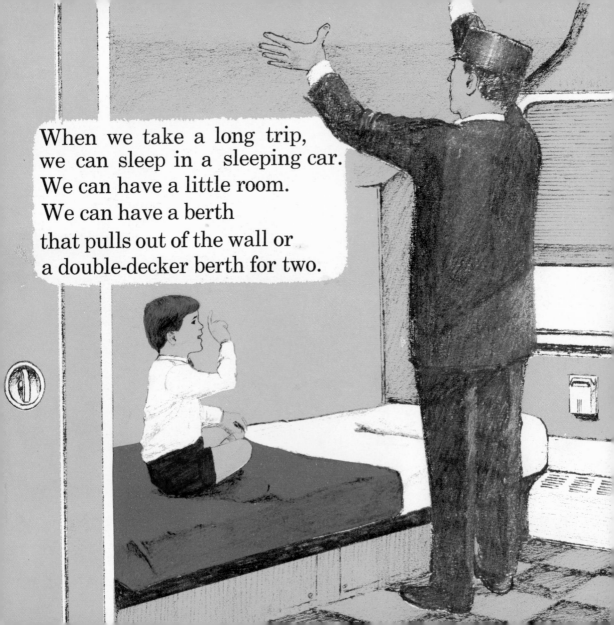

When we take a long trip,
we can sleep in a sleeping car.
We can have a little room.
We can have a berth
that pulls out of the wall or
a double-decker berth for two.

We can have a door, or a curtain that zips, to shut us snugly in. We have a button to call the porter. The porter takes care of us on the train.

We can lie in our berth and see the moon and houses where children are sleeping. The train rushes on through the night. The whistle cries, "Whoo-whoo!" The wheels say over and over again, "Chug-a-chug, chug-a-chug, chug-a-chug-chug."

We can walk through car after car when we take a long trip on the train. We can open the door of the car ourselves. "Psst," says the door.

Some trains have a dining car where we eat our dinner. Some trains have a lunch counter.

Some trains have machines where we buy our lunch. We put a dollar bill in a special place, and out come quarters and dimes. We drop our money in the slot. We take out a sandwich and milk. We can put our hamburgers into an oven that heats them in a few seconds.

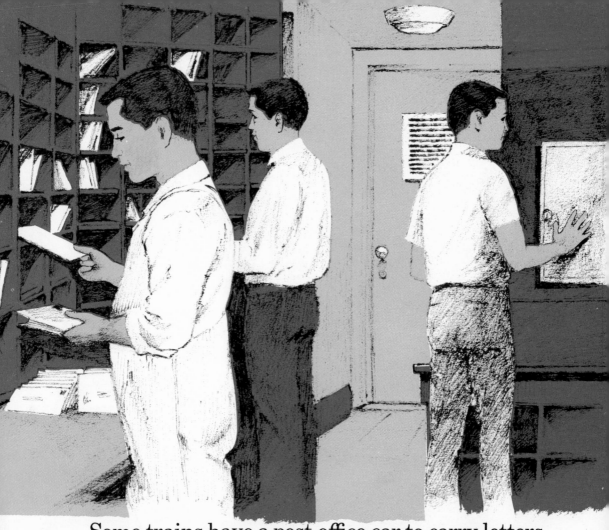

Some trains have a post-office car to carry letters to our grandma and grandpa and uncles and aunts and friends.

Some trains have double-decker cars.

Some trains have a dome car. We can climb the stairs

to the glass dome and get a good view of the scenery.

And on the end of some trains is an observation car. We can sit and look back at the places we pass. We can see the tracks go flying away from under the speeding wheels.

I *like* trains. . . .

All *kinds* of trains!